MW01222398

Busy Liz

by Helen Arnold

Illustrated by Tony Kenyon

A Piccolo Original
In association with Macmillan Education

Who lives here?

4

5

Len lives here.

Lazy Len.

Liz lives here, too.

Busy Liz.

Dad lives here, too.

Busy Liz.

Lazy Len.

Hurry up, Len.

Hurry up, Liz.

Busy Len.

Busy Len.

Lazy Liz!

Things to talk about with your children

1. The children in this story had to do a lot of things before they were ready for school. Can you remember some of the things they did?

2. Is it like that when you get up in the morning?
What's the same? What's different?

3. Do you think you are more like Liz or more like Len? Why?

Looking at the pictures and words
with your children

1. Can you find a page in the story where Liz is busy? Now can you find the page where she is lazy?

Can you find a page in the story where Len is lazy? Now can you find a page where he is busy?

2. Can you find the word lazy What letter does it begin with ? (Give the sound if the child doesn't know.)

Can you find the word busy What letter does it begin with ? (Give the sound if necessary.)

3. Do you know what time this is? (Tell the child if necessary.)

Can you find the picture of the clock which has the same time as this?
What was happening in the story then?

What time is this? Can you find it in the story?

What was happening in the story then?

4. What does this say? (Read it if necessary.)

Hurry up

Who said 'Hurry up' in the story?

Can you find all the times that Dad said Hurry up

Point to them. How many times did he say it?

Things for your child to do

1. Ask your child to put these pictures in the correct order, either by pointing to them in the order of the story, or by telling you about them.

2. Turn to the last page of the story. Talk to your children about what they think would happen next. Help them to make up a story to follow on from this last page.

These activities and skills:	will help your children to:
Looking and remembering	hold a story in their heads, retell it in their own words.
Listening, being able to tell the difference between sounds	remember sounds in words and link spoken words with the words they see in print.
Naming things and using different words to explain or retell events	recognise different words in print, build their vocabulary and guess at the meaning of words.
Matching, seeing patterns, similarities and differences	recognise letters, see patterns within words, use the patterns to read 'new' words and split long words into syllables.
Knowing the grammatical patterns of spoken language	guess the word-order in reading.
Anticipating what is likely to happen next in a story	guess what the next sentence or event is likely to be about.
Colouring, getting control of pencils and pens, copying and spelling	produce their own writing, which will help them to understand the way English is written.
Understanding new experiences by linking them to what they already know	read with understanding and think about what they have read.
Understanding their own feelings and those of others	enjoy and respond to stories and identify with the characters.

First published 1988 by Pan Books Ltd,
Cavaye Place, London SW10 9PG

9 8 7 6 5 4 3 2 1

Editorial consultant: Donna Bailey

© Pan Books Ltd and Macmillan Publishers Ltd
1988. Text © Helen Arnold 1988

British Library Cataloguing in Publication Data
Arnold, Helen
Busy Liz. — (Read together. Level 1).
I. Title II. Series
428.6   PE1119
ISBN 0–330–30211–6

Printed in Hong Kong

This book is sold subject to the condition that it
shall not, by way of trade or otherwise be lent,
re-sold, hired out or otherwise circulated
without the publisher's prior consent in any
form of binding or cover other than that in
which it is published and without a similar
condition including this condition being
imposed on the subsequent purchaser

Whilst the advice and information in this book
are believed to be true and accurate at the time
of going to press, neither the author nor the
publisher can accept any legal responsibility or
liability for any errors or omissions
that may be made